Original title:
Through the Ivy

Copyright © 2025 Creative Arts Management OÜ
All rights reserved.

Author: Henry Beaumont
ISBN HARDBACK: 978-1-80566-620-2
ISBN PAPERBACK: 978-1-80566-905-0

An Invitation from the Green

Come join the plants in noisy chat,
They gossip daily, this and that.
With leafy hats and snaky shoes,
They'll spin a tale of garden blues.

The daisies giggle, the roses tease,
While worms bring snacks with crafty ease.
A party brewed by sunshine bright,
Invite your friends, it's pure delight!

The Hidden Allure of the Wild

In the wild where secrets dwell,
Squirrels plot and nutters yell.
Beneath the bushes, mischief brews,
And chipmunks wear some silly shoes.

The trees sway to an unseen tune,
Dancing wildly beneath the moon.
Fairies laugh with leaves of jade,
A hidden world where jokes are made.

The Embrace of the Unseen

Shadows shuffle, what a sight!
They play in twilight, oh so light.
With every rustle, laughter rings,
As critters tease with silly flings.

A hidden hand that tickles trees,
The breeze whispers as it pleads.
In a world where magic brews,
The unseen dance in funny moods.

Polished Serenity in a Leafy Fold

Inside the fold where greens unite,
Laughter echoes, pure delight.
The ferns conclude their wavy casts,
While bugs debate on how to blast.

Sunbeams kiss the ground so fine,
A picnic's laid, it's grape and wine.
Join the fun, let worries fade,
In leafy realms where pranks are played.

Green Embers of Memory

In the garden, a gnome takes a snooze,
His pointy hat covered in morning dews.
Nearby, a squirrel dances with flair,
Mistaking my sandwich for a treasure rare.

The daisies giggle as the sun shines bright,
While the old oak tree sways with delight.
A worm in a bowtie declares with a cheer,
"I only eat dirt, but life's full of cheer!"

A Tapestry of Nature's Secrets

Lizards in hats trying to blend with the ground,
Plotting their schemes without making a sound.
A butterfly waves, says, "I'm late for tea!"
While the bees are buzzed up on honey and spree.

The flowers gossip while casting a glance,
At an ant in a tux, who's ready to dance.
As the breeze carries giggles in soft, leafy tones,
Nature's a party, where laughter's the bones.

The Maze of Botanical Dreams

In a maze made of vines, I took a wrong turn,
With a frog in a crown that began to learn.
"Here's a riddle!" he croaked, with a wink and a leap,
"What hops in the day and then takes a sleep?"

A ladybug chuckled, adorned with bright spots,
Sharing her secrets in scatterplot thoughts.
As the sun played tag with the shadows around,
Each corner revealed laughter where magic is found.

Memory's Verdant Embrace

Beneath leafy arches where shadows entwine,
A tiny frog floats in a jungle of brine.
He croaks out a tune that's delightfully wrong,
While lilies are swaying to nature's old song.

Worms in a circle are spinning a tale,
About a brave snail who set off on a trail.
With laughter like bubbles that rise in the air,
Memories dance softly, a whimsical flare.

Cravings for Emerald Haven

In the garden where the greenery sings,
Lizards dance with their tiny little wings,
Gnomes giggle, plotting their next prank,
While squirrels snack from the fountain's flank.

Underneath the leaves, a party brews,
The rabbits wear hats, each one in a fuse,
A raccoon juggles acorns in delight,
While fireflies spark like stars in the night.

A hedgehog in shades is sipping his tea,
While owls hoot jokes, as wise as can be,
The roses pop popcorn, the daisies just laugh,
As butterflies gossip about their next staff.

With each little critter, where nonsense prevails,
And laughter erupts on the leafy trails,
You'll find joy hiding where green shadows play,
In this emerald haven, come join the ballet.

Trails of Light through Leafy Gaps

Sunbeams dance with glee,
Chasing my toes, oh me!
A squirrel winks, quite spry,
As he dashes by, oh my!

Beneath the arch of green,
I trip on roots unseen.
Laughter echoes through the wood,
Who knew that I'd be good?

The Lure of Nature's Embrace

Leaves whisper secrets low,
Where mischief often flows.
A raccoon steals my snack,
Now I'm plotting my comeback!

Sunshine tickles my nose,
Nature's tease? Who knows!
Giggles rise past the trees,
Chasing shadows with the breeze.

Stories Hidden in the Green Veil

Beneath the leafy shade,
I find a lizard's parade.
They flick and flinch with flair,
As if they're debonair.

Fables told by the breeze,
Bring smiles with such ease.
Each rustling leaf a tale,
Of playful hearts that sail.

Currents of Whispers in Enclosed Spaces

In corners of the park,
Enter laughter, not a lark.
A mushroom sprouted wide,
It feels like nature's pride.

Sneaky squirrels dart fast,
With acorns unsurpassed.
They plot and plan with cheer,
For the nutty time of year.

The Sylvan Serenade

In the garden, squirrels dance,
Chasing shadows, lost in trance.
A rabbit in a silly hat,
Winks and hops, oh how he's fat.

Frogs sing loudly, on a quest,
Seeking flies, they jest and jest.
The trees giggle, leaves do sway,
As the sunbeams come to play.

Gnarly roots form a prankster's line,
Where a raccoon takes a little wine.
Birds trade jokes atop the boughs,
While butterflies perform their vows.

Laughter lingers in the air,
Nature's comedy, everywhere.
Underneath this leafy shroud,
Joy and whimsy, oh so loud.

Labyrinth of Lushness

In the maze of emerald dreams,
Caterpillars plot with devious themes.
A grasshopper strums, quite offbeat,
To the rhythm of fuzzy feet.

Honeybees buzz on a crusade,
Trading gossip in the glade.
A hedgehog rolls down the hill,
With acorns stacked, what a thrill!

Lizards bask in the sunlight's glow,
While crickets chirp their silly show.
Bramble bushes hide a prank,
As a wild fox gives a wink and thanks.

Joyful chaos, a wild spree,
In every leaf, a bit of glee.
With laughter bouncing from each nook,
Nature's charm, an open book.

Whispers in the Green Canopy

Sunlight filters through the leaves,
Squirrels plot with crafty thieves.
A parrot mimics every laugh,
Echoing nature's silly craft.

Beetles write love notes with care,
While flowers gossip, unaware.
A snail races without a rush,
In this leafy, giggling hush.

Breezes carry jests and sighs,
As a turtle rolls his eyes.
The forest floor, alive with cheer,
Whispers secrets only we hear.

A chorus forms, both loud and bright,
In the heart of the leafy light.
Nature's comedy, quite unique,
In the canopy, joy we seek.

Beneath a Tangle of Vines

Raccoons play hide and seek,
In the shadows, quick and sleek.
Under vines, a party blooms,
As curious bees hum gentle tunes.

Laughter weaves through every nook,
Where snakes curl up with a book.
A bunny tries to dance a jig,
While the owls tease, oh how they dig.

Twinking stars, fireflies play,
Lighting up the night in a fray.
Mice share tales, both tall and wide,
Finding fun where secrets hide.

Underneath this tangled green,
A silly world, fit for a queen.
With antics wild and hearts so free,
Nature's jesters, oh what glee!

The Quiet Sanctuary of Wandering Hearts

In whispers soft, we dodge the truth,
With giggles lost in adolescent sleuth.
A nook of dreams, where laughter bounces,
Among the leaves, our humor announces.

A squirrel chimes in, with jokes so grand,
While shadows play, a cheeky band.
We hide from fears, just me and you,
In this sanctuary, where hearts break through.

In the Stillness of the Garden Maze

With every turn, we paint a scene,
Dodging bushes, slipping between.
A butterfly laughs, as if to say,
Get lost a little, it's the perfect play.

The gnomes plot mischief, their grins so wide,
In the stillness, we giggle and glide.
Every petal whispers secrets low,
We trip on paths, yet never go slow.

The Mysterious Glow of Green Shadows

In twilight's grip, the moonlight plays,
While fireflies dance in a winking haze.
We venture forth, with caution and cheer,
Casting silly spells, nothing to fear.

A hedgehog peeks, with a curious stare,
What are you up to? Oh, simply rare.
Our giggles echo, a joyful glow,
Under the watch of the green shadow show.

Tomb of Secrets Suspended in Leaves

In this leafy tomb, stories slumber,
Of sandwich picnics and playful blunders.
We carve our names in bark so wise,
While old oak trees share their sighs.

A bumblebee buzzes, with gossip to spill,
Chasing our shadows with a cheerful thrill.
In this haven of mirth, we'll never cease,
To laugh at the world, it's a funny beast.

Veils of Green

Leaves do dance, they jig and sway,
Hiding secrets in a playful way.
Laughter echoes as squirrels pass,
Chasing shadows in the grass.

Vines wear hats of tangled glee,
Tickling toes of those who flee.
In the garden, fun unfolds,
With every smile, a tale retold.

Whispers Among the Vines

Grapes gossip, juicy and bold,
Sharing stories ages old.
Laughter bubbles from the ground,
As mischief in the leaves is found.

In the sun, the shadows play,
Tickling bees who drift away.
With every twist and every climb,
Nature's fun, a quirky rhyme.

Shadows in the Arbor

Under branches thick and wide,
Jokes are tossed like seeds in stride.
Silly faces made by dew,
Droplets giggle as they do.

Mice in suits roll down the lane,
Chasing dreams just like a train.
In the shade, the laughter flows,
Where whimsy thrives, and humor grows.

Beneath Canopy Dreams

In a world where ferns wear crowns,
Laughter blooms without the frowns.
Dancing shadows, swirling light,
Make each step a pure delight.

Beneath the greens, we find our cheer,
With every giggle, joy draws near.
Nature's jokes, so light and free,
Bring the heart a sweet decree.

Echoes of Nature's Lattice

In a garden where things twist and weave,
The plants gossip and no one believes.
A snail told a joke, it slid with a grin,
While bees buzzed along, thick as a din.

With vines that dance, and roots that tap,
A squirrel lost his acorn, fell in a flap.
Oh, nature's comedy is never too shy,
Just ask the poor bird that learned how to fly.

The flowers chuckle, petals a-flutter,
A wise old frog, who dreams of peanut butter.
They tease the poor branch that leans far away,
Saying it daydreams of becoming a tray.

But in this wild show, all's playful and jest,
Even the weeds think they're better than zest.
So pause for a moment, let laughter take root,
In the green tapestry, truth's kinda a hoot.

Hidden Realms of the Climbing Green

Look close and you'll find a leafy parade,
Where spiders are kings, though none would invade.
The ladybugs giggle, the ants hold a chat,
While a butterfly lands, looking quite fat.

A wily old vine with its twirls and bends,
Claims it's the master, the queen of best friends.
While mushrooms hold court on a damp wooden log,
Voting for the title of 'Best Insect Fog.'

In this bustling world of green, bright delight,
Even the shadows are planning a flight.
With larks in the chorus, they sing out in glee,
Just dodging the raindrops that mess up their spree.

So venture with laughter, let whimsy abound,
In the secretive realms where funny quirks sound.
Each branch plays a part, a joyful charade,
In the tangled comedy nature has made.

Ensnared by the Lush Veil

In the thickets where silliness thrives,
The grass claims it's hosting a party of hives.
A raccoon in shades serves berry delight,
While the fireflies flash like the stars in the night.

The whispering leaves are the gossiping sort,
Telling tall tales of a squirrel's last sport.
He leaped for a twig but landed askew,
On a porcupine's back, oh what a view!

With bumbles and tumbles, the critters collide,
Chasing their tails on the green slides they ride.
A hedgehog grins wide, while rolling away,
Saying "Life's just a game, come join in play."

So dive into laughter, let nature unfold,
In this lush enchanted, where tales are retold.
Every twist and each turn, a chuckle unfurls,
In the wild tangled mess of this green, funny world.

Where Foliage Meets the Sky

Up high in the branches, the birds have a ball,
Chasing the clouds although missing the call.
A crow cracks a joke, while the blue jay just laughs,
At the squirrel who's stuck, caught between halves.

The trees push and shuffle, their leaves all in play,
As the sunlight chuckles, brightening the day.
A chipmunk sings out with a voice brave and bold,
Telling tales of the nuttiest things he's been told.

With shadows that dance, and sunlight that winks,
The foliage giggles, oh how brightly it shrinks.
A sweet little fern, with a feathery sway,
Claims it's the star of the greenery play.

So peek into this paradise, free of all sighs,
Let the laughter of nature dance into your eyes.
In the moments of whimsy, in tangled delight,
Find joy in the greenery, pure fun in the light.

Treading Old Earth

I walked on soil, felt it squish,
Found a worm who made a wish.
He twirled around, doing the cha-cha,
'Hey, watch me dance!' he said, 'Fla-la!'

A squirrel nearby stole my snack,
Gave a wink, then made a crack.
He chattered loud, with nuts in hand,
'Join my crew, we're a wild band!'

Nature plays on this old stage,
Laughs with the winds, turns the page.
Even the ants, they hold a feast,
With tiny hats, they're quite the beast!

So if you stroll on this soft ground,
And hear strange sounds that dance around,
Just smile and nod, don't take a leap,
For even worms have secrets to keep!

Clusters of Serendipity

Beneath the vines where daisies gleam,
A bee got lost in a daydream.
He buzzed and hummed, quite out of tune,
'Can someone tell me—where's my noon?'

Where sunflowers wear a golden crown,
A ladybug in a polka gown,
Sipped nectar like it was the best wine,
Said, 'In this garden, I truly shine!'

The hedgehogs threw a garden bash,
With tiny flags and lots of trash.
Their music played from a broken box,
While they danced out, wearing odd socks!

So tiptoe through, embrace the jest,
On every leaf, a funny quest.
With nature's quirks all on display,
You'll leave with laughs and bright bouquet!

Pathways of Petals

In gardens where the shadows play,
I found a snail who lost his way.
He squirmed around with such great pride,
'Excuse me ma'am, I'm on a ride!'

A flower whispered, 'Hey, slow down!'
'You're cruising fast, why not lie down?
The sun is warm, it's pure delight,
Let's talk about the moon at night!'

A group of frogs began to croak,
Telling tales in a smoky cloak.
'The flies we caught made quite a stew,
Come join us, bring your favorite brew!'

So if you wander by this scene,
Embrace each leaf, and laugh between.
For in the petals and the grass,
You'll find fun moments, let them pass!

Shadows Forged by Green Light

Beneath the boughs, a shadow danced,
A gopher twirled, he took a chance.
'Bet you can't do this neat trick!'
He rolled and flipped, a little quick!

A hedgerow chat, with quips and puns,
The rabbits laughed, they're always fun.
'Tell us more!' they squealed with glee,
'About your wacky escapade spree!'

The bushes rustled with a cheer,
A fox showed up without a fear.
He tipped his hat, then pranced around,
'In this green world, joy has been found!'

So walk along this verdant trail,
With each shadow, let laughter sail.
For in this grove of leafy play,
The joy of nature lights the way!

Serenity within the Green Embrace

In the garden where the rabbits feast,
Wearing tiny hats, like a showbiz beast.
They sip on nectar, laugh and dance,
While bees in tuxedos take a chance.

The flowers gossip in vibrant hues,
Swapping tales of the latest snooze.
With petals fluttering like a fan,
They dream of becoming a rockstar band.

Squirrels play chess, all fur and flair,
Arguing who wins, we simply stare.
The pond reflects a silly grin,
As frogs croak songs—let the fun begin!

Amidst this joy of leafy cheer,
The whispers of laughter fill the air.
So grab a snack, don't mind the mess,
In this green sanctum, we are truly blessed.

Beneath the Canopy's Guard

Beneath the branches, secrets hide,
A hedgehog's dance is full of pride.
With twirls and spins, so sly and spry,
He twitches his nose, oh my, oh my!

The whispers chuckle, leaves overhead,
As ants hold meetings, seriously said.
With tiny briefcases, they march in line,
Debating crumbs like it's divine.

A robin sings in the grandest key,
Crooning about bugs as his main spree.
While chipmunks barter with acorn bling,
What a delight their antics bring!

Laughter ricochets, oh what a show,
Beneath this shelter, joy takes tow.
So join the fun in this lively charade,
In nature's circus, let's all upgrade!

The Color of Enchantment

In colors bright, the hues collide,
A parrot struts, full of pride.
His feathered cap, an eye-popping shade,
With laughter sparkles, his antics played.

The daisies giggle, the violets blush,
A sunbeam's tickle causes a rush.
They sway with glee as the breeze unfolds,
In this patch of whimsy, laughter molds.

Caterpillars wear their best bow ties,
Dreaming of wings under sunny skies.
They chat of fashion while munching leaves,
In this vibrant world, joy never leaves.

Dancing with colors, spirits so light,
Each shade a joke, oh what a sight!
Join this palette of bliss and cheer,
Where laughter glows, and smiles appear.

Harvesting Light from the Shadows

In the twilight where shadows play,
A squirrel devises a daring ballet.
With leaps and bounds, he's full of glee,
His tiny top hat, quite the sight to see!

The night bugs rave, they're dressed so fine,
In sparkly coats, they dance in line.
They jive under moonlight's gentle beam,
Creating rhythms like a sweet dream.

The stars giggle, twinkling with flair,
As glowworms gather, causing a stare.
They glow like lanterns, a party bright,
In this quirky realm, they own the night!

What fun it is to laugh and play,
When shadows bring magic at end of day.
So join the frolic, let your heart soar,
In this world of whimsy, you'll find much more!

A Tapestry of Leaf and Light

In the garden, leaves collide,
A tapestry where critters hide.
Squirrels chatter, frogs croak loud,
Nature's party, oh so proud.

Bumblebees wearing tiny hats,
Dancing to the sound of chitchat.
Sunlight giggles, shadows play,
Grass stains on clothes, what a day!

Lizards sunbathing on the stones,
Whisper secrets in funny tones.
Every leaf's a story spun,
In this realm of leafy fun.

Come and laugh with all the critters,
Join the fun, no room for quitters.
A leaf's a slide, a petal's a seat,
Nature's joy, oh, what a treat!

Starlit Vines and Moonlit Paths

Under stars, the vines entwine,
Moonlit roads where shadows dine.
Owls wear spectacles, all aglow,
Judging the mice putting on a show.

Raccoons with masks, they steal the scene,
Taking snacks from a trash can queen.
Fireflies flash in goofy glee,
Lighting up the night, just wait and see!

Wrapped in vines, a cat's lost track,
Ignores the world, just wants a snack.
Wandering paths with no real plan,
Witty wanderers forming a clan.

Join the fun in starry night,
Where moonlit vines bring pure delight.
Every rustle makes you grin,
In this wild world, we all win!

In the Heart of the Leafy Labyrinth

In a thicket where paths get lost,
Giggles echo, oh what a cost!
Bushes whisper silly confessions,
Every step, a new obsession.

In this maze, the bees are buzzing,
With flowery plans, they're never fussing.
Pigeons practicing their roguish dance,
Nature's quirks, the quirkiest chance.

A hedgehog wiggles, wearing a crown,
While passing squirrels just frown.
The foolish fern sways to a tune,
Dripping dew drops like a monsoon.

So spin and twirl, join the spree,
In leafy lanes of pure decree.
Laughter rings where secrets creep,
In this jungle, fun runs deep!

Nature's Woven Secrets

In the garden, secrets bloom,
Woven tales break the gloom.
Dandelions with their puffed-up pride,
Hoping for wishes, they all collide.

With giggles and puffs, they float away,
Wondering if they'll be back someday.
Spiders spin their webs of fun,
Trapping laughter just like sun.

Beneath the branches, owls hold court,
Warbling stories with no retort.
Every nut and berry tells a joke,
In this whimsical woodland cloak.

So join the dance of nature's thrives,
In these woods where true joy dives.
From hidden roots to leafy tops,
Unlocking laughter that never stops!

Fluttering Dreams Behind the Vines

A butterfly slipped on a slick, green shoe,
It danced with the breezes, as if it knew.
With giggles and wiggles, it zoomed here and there,
Jumped into a daisy, without any care.

A rabbit nearby wore a hat quite absurd,
It wobbled and bobbed with each little word.
Said, "Chase after dreams or you'll end up like me,
Stuck in a garden, as nutty as can be!"

The sun tickled leaves and the shadows would play,
As creatures conspired to jazz up the day.
They plotted and planned a wild, silly feast,
With snacks made of daisies and grasshopper yeast.

And when the night came, oh, what a delight!
The stars popped like popcorn, a dazzling sight.
So gather your dreams and be vague and whine,
In gardens mysterious, let your heart shine!

Boughs of Whispering Secrets

The big old oak laughed with a creaking sound,
    Telling the tales of the critters around.
A squirrel wearing glasses was writing a book,
About how to hide when a hawk comes to look.

The branches were busy, exchanging sweet tricks,
To keep the birds safe from their sneaky old picks.
"Don't trust the crows," whispered leaves in a breeze,
"They'll snack on your lunch and then beg you for keys!"

A chipmunk proclaimed with a puffed-up chest,
"I'm the king of this forest, you'll find me the best!"
But when he sat down, he got stuck in a pot,
And everyone giggled, he was not quite so hot.

In the moonlight's glow, laughter echoed so wide,
As secrets were shared, the woods swelled with pride.
Embrace the absurd in the haven of trees,
Where whispers are jokes on the night's gentle breeze.

An Odyssey Through Nature's Veil

A hedgehog set sail on a leaf that could float,
With dreams of a beach and a big rubber boat.
It paddled with passion, a true little ace,
Until a frog croaked, "You've got mud on your face!"

The flowers held court with opinions in bloom,
"Who wears the best petals? Who's meeting their doom?"

With laughter and giggles, they tallied each score,
When a butterfly swooped in and started to roar!

A raccoon named Benny brought pie to the show,
Said, "Sweet as a dream is this blueberry flow!"
But when he was caught just raiding the stash,
The crowd burst with giggles, his pride turned to ash.

Through bushes and brambles, a tall tale was spun,
Of adventures and mishaps, of splashes and fun.
So come take a trip with each slip and each fail,
In the wild little world, weaved in Nature's veil.

The Hidden Messages of Leaves

Each leaf had a story, a message to share,
Whispered by breezes that floated through air.
"Don't step on my friend, the worm in the ground!"
Said one little maple, who wobbled around.

A sycamore grinned, showing off all its bark,
"Come gather 'round folks, let's lighten the dark!"
With jokes about squirrels and things that they stole,
The laughter erupted, it brightened each soul.

The willows took note of the giggles they heard,
They started to sway, as if they concurred.
"Let's throw a party with all of the trees,
And dance 'neath the starlight with laughter and ease!"

So gather your pals, let the leaves have their say,
In this forest of secrets, let fun lead the way.
There's joy in the rustle, a grin in each shade,
For nature's big heart is a party well made!

Where Shadows Dance with Light

In a realm where sunlight weaves,
Laughter echoes through the leaves.
Squirrels play in acorn suits,
While worms wear ties and tiny boots.

The shadows giggle as they prance,
In a dappled, leafy dance.
A breeze whispers silly jokes,
Tickling the noses of the oaks.

Lizards bask with cheeky grins,
As butterflies cheer for their wins.
Frogs in bow ties croak their tune,
Competing with a silly raccoon.

Nature spins a playful tale,
With trees that waltz and flowers sail.
So come and join the merry throng,
In this delightfully wacky song.

A Journey Through Nature's Tapestry

A path where colors twist and twine,
The flowers gossip, oh so fine.
Rabbits zoom in hopscotch games,
While hedgehogs share their funny names.

The sun wears shades, so cool and nice,
As chipmunks snack on peanut rice.
A tapestry of giggles bright,
Stitched with patches of pure delight.

Treetops bow in playful glee,
While ants debate their grand decree.
With nature's laughter all around,
In this joy, true peace is found.

So let's embrace this silly spree,
And dance along, just you and me.
In every rustle, in every sound,
A journey of fun will always abound.

Enveloped by the Lush Embrace

In velvety greens where giggles rise,
The flowers form a winking surprise.
Beetles sport their tiny hats,
While ladybugs play with the chitchats.

Beneath the trees, shadows collide,
Nature's humor, it can't hide.
A playful breeze whispers loud and clear,
Jokes bounce around for all to hear.

The brook chuckles, splashes with cheer,
As frogs join in with a big loud cheer.
Vines tango with the breezy air,
In this fun-filled leafy lair.

So gather round in this lively space,
Unravel that smile and embrace.
Amidst the greenery's playful chase,
Welcome to joy's delightful place!

The Third Dimension of Green

In a world where green goes beyond,
Giggles sprout in every pond.
Llamas wear capes, on hills they lounge,
With woodland creatures all around.

A kaleidoscope of silly sights,
Where hedgehogs juggle, delighting bites.
The mossy carpet whispers fun,
As snails race under the warm sun.

Beneath the canopy, secrets hide,
As squirrels spin tales with countryside pride.
Every branch holds a laughing tune,
As critters dance 'neath the smiling moon.

So come and roam this vibrant scheme,
Where nature lives and laughs, it seems.
In this lush realm of mirth and play,
Every step brings a brighter day.

Sunlight Dappled Mystery

In a garden where shadows play,
The sunbeams dance, bright as may.
Squirrels frolic, chasing dreams,
While birds converse in silly themes.

A gnome grins wide, holding a shoe,
Whispers secrets, just a view.
While daisies giggle, a rosy hue,
And butterflies wear hats askew.

A cat with style strolls by charm,
With swagger that causes alarm.
He stops for a sip, a playful pause,
Now that's one bizarre cause!

A hedgehog hums a tune so fine,
Using vines as a makeshift line.
As laughter echoes, honeybees buzz,
This garden's charm, it surely does!

The Enchanted Pergola

Beneath the shade, the laughter swells,
In a maze of leaves, a tale compels.
Rabbits host a tea-time spree,
With pastries served on a bumblebee.

A couple of snails have brought a snack,
While ants march on in a quirky pack.
The toad plays cards, down to the wire,
With a sly grin, he cheats with fire!

The ivy climbs, with mischief clear,
Wrapping up woes with every cheer.
As garden gnomes break into a dance,
All join in, giving fun a chance!

A chameleon dons a vibrant hat,
Winking at each curious cat.
With petals flying like confetti bright,
In this leafy realm, all feels just right!

Lattice of Forgotten Stories

In whispers soft among the vines,
Lie tales of fruits and secret signs.
A squirrel spills a nutty joke,
While shadows weave as laughter spoke.

A parrot claims he's quite the star,
With antics that raise the bizarre.
The spiders spin their silken thread,
Hoping to host a stand-up spread.

A ladybug with polka dots,
Proclaims her fame in happy spots.
While beetles join a conga line,
This hollyhock plays the sunshine!

Rooted tales speak of mishaps grand,
Like when the tree forgot to stand.
Yet through it all, the laughter flows,
In every leaf, a joy that grows!

Vines that Bind the Past

Twists and turns of leafy fate,
Entwined in laughter, never late.
A snail recounts his days so bold,
While fables of friends are retold.

The owls hoot tunes of old-day charms,
Beneath the leaves, in open arms.
With frogs that croak their punchline fate,
In this thicket, humor's great!

A raccoon sneaks with sticky paws,
Snatching snacks with cheeky claws.
While playful breezes ruffle tales,
Of every critter's wondrous wails.

So here's to vines that make us grin,
Binding stories, thick and thin.
For in this leafy, happy place,
Each moment shines with joy and grace!

A Journey Beneath the Foliage

In the shade of tangled greens,
A raccoon dances, no in-betweens.
He trips on roots, looks quite perplexed,
A comedy show, nature's context.

Leaves whisper secrets, giggles unfold,
A squirrel's antics, brash and bold.
He hoards acorns, but what a sight,
As they roll away—what a delight!

Beneath the canopy, shadows play,
With whispers of mischief, come what may.
Chasing sunlight, they make their way,
In nature's jest, they dance and sway.

So let's join the fun, let go of fears,
And laugh with the leaves, as nature cheers.
In this leafy world, let joy reside,
As we prance along, what a wild ride!

Breaths of Fresh Green Wishes

Amidst the ferns, two frogs compete,
For the finest lily pad seat.
One leaps high with style and flair,
The other plops with a splash of air.

Whimsical winds tickle the broccoli,
As bugs hold court in a goofy decree.
They laugh and chatter, they sing and sway,
As the blooms giggle in the sunny play.

In this garden realm, delight erupts,
With butterflies swirling, and cream puffs.
A ladybug twirls in a dizzy spree,
While caterpillars plot a climb, oh me!

With every step, a jest unfolds,
A tapestry woven with laughter bold.
So take a breath of fresh green air,
And join the whimsy, let's share a care!

The Cloistered Journey of Vines

Vines twirl together in comical dance,
Planting their feet, giving it a chance.
They sway with the breeze in playful yells,
As berries pop out, casting their spells.

A chubby worm on a leafy spree,
Wobbles and giggles quite carelessly.
While leafy friends hold their breath tight,
Waiting for him to take a flight!

Tangles of green with a snapshot glee,
Creating a ruckus, what sight to see!
The moonlight chuckles as dawn takes a peek,
At the mischief found in each glossy creek.

So let's journey down this leafy lane,
With vines holding hands, oh what joy to gain!
Let laughter be our leafy crown,
As we tumble and roll with vines all around!

Hues of Serendipity in Leafy Darkness

In twilight's cloak, a dance unfolds,
With creatures bold and stories told.
A possum jigs, oh what a sight,
In hues of mischief, he takes flight!

Fireflies twinkle, dressed up in dreams,
While rabbits hold court, or so it seems.
Chasing shadows beyond the dark,
With wild antics that hit the spark.

Mushrooms chuckle, their caps aglow,
As laughter spills in a leafy show.
With whimsy dripping from every stem,
Every twist and turn, an unseen gem!

So blend in with hues that soon will sway,
In this leafy riddle, come dance and play.
With mischief and joy, let spirits soar,
As we bask in colors that we adore!

Between Roots and Sunlit Dreams

Beneath the tangled vines we play,
Chasing shadows that dart and sway.
With gnarled roots that trip our feet,
We laugh as we tumble, oh what a feat!

Sunlit beams peek in between,
Painting faces with a gleam.
Each giggle echoes through the leaves,
As nature dances, and mischief weaves.

A squirrel sneaks up with a nut in tow,
We freeze in place, then we all go 'whoa!'
A slip, a trip, and down it falls,
And now it's a feast for the birds' loud calls.

So here we are, a merry band,
In this leafy realm so unplanned.
With every twist and wobbly glide,
Life's a joyful, bouncy ride!

The Whispering Canopy Above

Under the leafy arch we sneak,
Giggles dance like a playful creek.
The branches sway and start to chat,
'Who's that down there? They're quite flat!'

A bird roars laughter from the bough,
As clumsy friends take a seat now.
We sink down deep, oh what a sight,
With ivy crowns, we feel just right!

Clouds peek down, oh what a grin,
They whisper jokes as they spin and spin.
'Knock knock!' one says from the above,
'Who's there?' we shout, a game we love!

So let the branches sway and twist,
In this world, how could we resist?
With every giggle and verdant cheer,
We find our joy in nature's sphere!

Enigma of the Green Shell

In the garden's secret nook we find,
A shell of green, so unrefined.
We ponder on what it contains,
Perhaps a frog or some playful rains!

A bustle of bugs, they peek and poke,
"What's in there?" we giggle and joke.
A snail zooms past with a wink,
'No peeking, friends, or you'll sink!'

As we lean in to take a glance,
Something inside starts to dance!
With a shake and a wiggle, oh dear me,
Out pops a rabbit, wild and free!

So here in this riddle of green delight,
We share our wonder, laughing bright.
For in every shell, a story we find,
Unveiling laughter, so sweet and kind!

Cradle of Foliage Dreams

In the cradle where the leaves all sway,
We spin our tales, come join the play!
Soft whispers pass from branch to branch,
As we giggle and wiggle in a leafy dance.

Dirt on our shoes, but smiles so wide,
In this world, we have nothing to hide.
A ladybug joins our silly spree,
'What's the secret?' It asks with glee!

With every twist and twirl we take,
The ivy giggles and starts to quake.
Tiny fairies peek from the glade,
Waving their wands, in sunlight played.

So let us frolic, let us beam,
In this cradle of foliage dreams.
For every leaf and every beam,
Recites fond tales that make us beam!

Surrender to the Enveloping Green

In a garden where laughter grows,
A leaf tickles a nose, oh such woes!
The vines dance like a spirited crew,
Whispering secrets that only they knew.

With every twist, I'm caught in a bind,
Nature's embrace is so wildly unkind,
A frog leaps over with a ribbiting cheer,
As I tumble into a bush, vanishing near.

The petals giggle as bees buzz around,
Spinning tales of mischief, no ending found,
I trip on the roots, but it's all in good fun,
A day spent in greenery can't be outdone!

In leafy laughter, I find my release,
Nature's comedy makes my worries cease,
So here in the green, I shall stay like a fool,
For life is a joke, and nature's the school!

The Avenues of Nature's Hand

Wandering pathways where branches sway,
I duck from a branch that's here for the play,
With foliage weaving a whimsical maze,
Each turn leads to laughter, a humorous phase.

A squirrel dons acorns like fashion's best wear,
While I shuffle below, with style less than rare,
Moss cushions my fall, it's a soft, green embrace,
Yet my shoes betray me in this slip 'n' race.

The wind plays a tune, quite catchy, you'll see,
While leaves applaud, oh so sprightly, with glee,
I bumble and tumble, an intricate dance,
Nature's comedy truly gives life a chance!

In the midst of it all, joy plants its seed,
For adventures may stumble, but laughter's the need,
A symphony of chuckles entwined with the bark,
Here in the hands of the trees, I find spark!

In the Heart of Wild Embrace

A vine wraps around, oh what a delight,
As I play peek-a-boo with a worm in the night,
He chuckles so loudly, I'm starting to brag,
As plants joke and jive, my sides start to sag.

With petals for pillows, I nestle and sigh,
While chattering critters buzz by with a why,
Nature's buffet offers laughter galore,
But I swallow a bug—now what's in store?

The dance of the daisies is quite a wild sight,
As they whirl and they twirl underneath the moonlight,
A snail's slow parade makes headlines today,
In the heart of this wild, oh what fun to play!

So here let me linger, let merriment grow,
With blooms that provide the finest of show,
In this vibrant embrace, the wild does impart,
A symphony charming, it tugs at the heart!

Wanderlust Amongst Climbing Flora

With every step taken, a vine gives a cheer,
"Get tangled with us!" they seem to declare near,
While laughter erupts from the petals in view,
Each joke that they tell surely gets better too.

I stumbled on roots that had dreams of their own,
Competing for giggles, they have fully grown,
And ferns burst out laughing, their fans in full roar,
As I dance like a penguin, they crave for encore!

Bumblebees hum tunes, in-sync to the breeze,
While butterflies nap, cozy under trees,
Nature's own circus unfolds all around,
In this blossoming world, pure humor is found.

So here in the greenery, let troubles unwind,
Let nature's punchlines cheerfully remind,
That laughter is planted like seeds in the air,
In a wanderlust heart, let's frolic and share!

Echoes in the Garden

In the garden, whispers roam,
Where gnomes gossip, far from home.
A snail debates a creeping vine,
While ladybugs dance, sipping wine.

The daisies laugh at the weeds' plight,
Who think they can join the pretty sight.
Frogs croak jokes in the moon's embrace,
As fireflies flash—a light-hearted race.

A cat, in stealth, plots its next prank,
While ants march by, in a neat little rank.
The petals giggle, the grass will sway,
In this silly garden, come what may.

So tiptoe carefully, don't break the spell,
In this merry patch where all critters dwell.
From time to time, just stop for a chuckle,
And join in the fun, where laughter will buckle.

Gossamer Threads of Nature

In the morning dew, reflections gleam,
Spiders weave tales, or so it would seem.
A beetle struts in a tuxedo fine,
While butterflies giggle at his bold line.

Ladybugs twirl in a joyous ballet,
While the grasshoppers cheer from their stage of hay.
A worm writes poems, or so he pretends,
While caterpillars claim they've got all the trends.

Clouds float by, making silly faces,
While squirrels chase dreams in chaotic races.
"Why did the branch break?" giggles the tree,
"Because it couldn't bear all the laughs, you see!"

With gossamer threads, the day spins around,
In whimsy and giggles, true joy can be found.
So join in the laughter, don't let it flee,
Nature's a jester—come, dance with me!

Hidden in the Hedges

In the hedges, secrets hide,
As rabbits laugh and squirrels bide.
A fox with a hat tells tall tales,
While hedgehogs try on their tiny veils.

A secret club of grass and clover,
Plans silly pranks, a playful takeover.
"Knock knock!" chirps the robin, with glee,
"Who's there?" says the leaf, beneath the tree.

Tangled in laughter, the blooms all sway,
As bees and bugs plan their wild fête day.
A loud snap! A twig's broken in jest,
The laughter erupts—who's the best dressed?

Underneath the twilight, a party unfolds,
With tales of brave gnomes and glittering gold.
Join the mischief, embrace the charade,
In the hedges, every giggle is made!

Lanterns of the Leafy Realm

Beneath the leaves, where shadows play,
Glow lanterns bright, in a whimsical way.
Fireflies gossip, spark a new trend,
With every buzz, they light up and bend.

A raccoon in boots, a hat on his head,
Dances with daisies, oh, joyfully led!
The wind makes wishes, like whispers of charms,
As trees tell stories with open, wide arms.

Silly old owls hoot riddled laughs,
While toadstools chuckle in circular staffs.
A party of petals, where smiles ignite,
In the leafy realm, all hearts feel light.

So twirl with the lanterns, follow their lead,
In this world of giggles, come plant a seed.
Let laughter be roots, in the soil so deep,
In the leafy realm, where joy never sleeps!

To Wander Under Canopies

Amid the leaves, the squirrels play,
Chasing shadows, they dart away.
A rabbit sneezes, much to my shock,
As I trip over my mismatched socks.

The sun peeks through with a goofy grin,
While birds debate who starts to sing.
They chirp and squawk, in a funny fight,
The randomness of nature feels just right.

I wonder if ants ever dream of flight,
Or if grasshoppers juggle in the moonlight.
Underneath the trees, life's a grand play,
And I'm just the fool who lost their way.

But laughter blooms in every green nook,
In this wild world, there's no need to book.
With every step, surprises unroll,
As nature giggles, and I lose control.

Nature's Whispered Memoirs

In the quiet hush of fluttering leaves,
A raccoon muses, mischief it weaves.
Each branch a story, a giggle, a tale,
Of fuzzy fellas who remarkably fail.

The daisies chatter with bees in the sun,
While worms claim the soil—it's all in good fun.
Clouds dance in circles, let out a cheer,
"Why don't we play hide and seek here?"

The squirrels make bets on who'll fall first,
While chortling frogs quench their big thirst.
The river chuckles with a bubbly flow,
In nature's laughter, joy seems to grow.

Tales of old trees spin in the breeze,
As I stumble along like I'm walking on cheese.
With pebbles that giggle, and shadows that play,
Nature's memoirs brighten my day.

Vistas Behind the Foliage

Peeking 'round bushes, what do I see?
A hedgehog pondering, sipping his tea.
Behind leafy curtains, the antics unfold,
Where laughter and stories are endlessly told.

Dancing in sunlight, the butterflies flirt,
While crickets recite poetry in dirt.
A raccoon critiques the local cuisine,
As bees waltz gracefully, a charming scene.

And there by the stream, puddles ripple with chat,
Where fish practice diving—imagine that!
Each splash creates giggles, a watery prank,
In this hidden world, there's no need to thank.

The wild ways of creatures, they never deceive,
They bloom with humor, oh, what to believe!
As I watch from behind, in a leafy brigade,
I chuckle at life on this grand escapade.

The Curls of Lost Letters

Worn letters drift on the breeze, oh so sly,
Whispering secrets as they flutter by.
A worm takes a nibble, "Is this even prose?"
While insects debate what the true meaning knows.

The postman's a fox, delivering glee,
With jokes in his pouch, what silliness we see!
Each stamp a treasure, each envelope a grin,
As squirrels deliver mail with a twirl and a spin.

In tangled vines, the laughter erupts,
Where frogs read the mail and delightfully corrupt.
They snicker and ribbit, "What a foolish plight!"
In this curious chaos, everything's bright.

Under the foliage, stories collide,
In nature's lost letters, we find joy inside.
Embracing the funny, wild, and absurd,
These curls of old laughter, forever heard.

In the Shelter of Nature's Arms

I found a leaf, it waved at me,
A squirrel danced, so wild and free.
Beneath the trees, I heard a shout,
"Watch your head! There's acorns about!"

A rabbit hopped, with quite the flair,
Wearing glasses, it seemed so rare.
With every twist, the branches creaked,
Nature's jokes, oh how they peaked!

A wise old owl, perched up high,
Said, "Why do leaves always seem shy?"
Just then a breeze blew, soft and cool,
And tickled noses like a fool!

In nature's arms, the laughter swells,
With whispered tales, and funny spells.
So come join in, don't miss the fun,
Under the sky, we're all just one!

Echoes Between the Layers of Green

Amid the ferns, a raccoon laughed,
He stole a snack, oh what a craft!
The leaves were rustling, secrets spoke,
A toad croaked loud, a naughty joke.

A parrot squawked, "Why so glum?"
Just then, a bug went 'pop' and 'thrum'.
Laughter echoed through the thick,
A worm wiggled, and did a trick!

"Guess who's next?" a frog did tease,
His flip was bold,; he soared with ease.
The greenwood chimed in joyous cheer,
Nature's laughter, always near.

So come on down, beneath the green,
Where funny faces can be seen.
Every shadow has a grin,
In layers deep, the fun begins!

The Path where Light Kisses Shade

Along the path where shadows play,
I met a gnome who lost his way.
He wore a hat, all bright and bold,
And told me tales of treasures untold.

"Don't step on ferns!" he gave a yell,
"They're full of giggles, can't you tell?"
With every step, the sun would dance,
As critters joined in, what a prance!

A fox in shades was plotting schemes,
While sunbeams tangled in my dreams.
With every twist and turn I take,
The light and shade began to shake!

So walk with me, let laughter bloom,
As sunlight brightens every room.
The path we share, where giggles reign,
In shadowed delight, there's no more pain!

Heartbeats Beneath the Canopy

The trees were swaying, beats like drums,
While chipmunks danced, in tiny slums.
I giggled loud, my heart so light,
As nature's party kicked off that night.

"Come join the fun!" a cicada cried,
With claps that echoed, oh so wide.
The stars above blinked jealous eyes,
As fireflies twinkled, the night skies.

A bear appeared, and started to sway,
His dancing style? A fresh ballet.
With paws so big, and moves so slick,
He spun around — oh, what a trick!

Beneath this canopy, life's a jest,
Where laughter chirps, we're truly blessed.
So take a seat, and join the spree,
In heartbeats shared, wild and free!

A Symphony of Twining Trails

In the garden, vines do dance,
Tangled legs in a leafy prance.
A squirrel laughs, it's all a game,
Critters join in, but who's to blame?

A twist, a turn, what's next to spring?
A caterpillar who likes to sing.
The colors swirl, a brilliant show,
Even the flowers put on a glow.

Unraveled in the Thicket

In the bramble, lost we'll be,
Chasing shadows, what's that tree?
A rabbit giggles, hops in delight,
Leaves tickle noses, what a sight!

We search for paths that aren't even real,
Stumble and tumble, that's the deal.
With a chuckle, we wave at a bee,
'Can you lead us, oh busy one? Plea!

Silhouettes of Wandering Souls

Figures flit in the fading light,
Dancing shadows, what a fright!
A raccoon winks, what's this caper?
Laughter echoes, gets the paper!

Through the grove, we skip and sway,
The path is messy, don't care today.
A chorus of giggles, that's our song,
Vines entwined, can't be wrong!

Veils of Ivy and Time

Time tick-tocks, as ivy clings,
Nature's humor, oh how it sings!
A gnome wobbles on a crooked chair,
Join the fun, if you dare!

Whispers of laughter tucked away,
In leafy nooks, we'll gladly stay.
With silly hats and giggles loud,
We'll reign in our leafy crowd!

www.ingramcontent.com/pod-product-compliance
Lightning Source LLC
Chambersburg PA
CBHW071827160426
43209CB00003B/216